Jack Hasling

FOOTPRINTS
ON MY
TONGUE

Outskirts Press, Inc.
Denver, Colorado

Footprints On My Tongue
All Rights Reserved
Copyright © 2007 Jack Hasling
Vr1.0

Outskirts Press
http://www.outskirtspress.com

ISBN-10: -1-59800-633-9
ISBN-13: 978-1-59800-633-9

Outskirts Press and the "OP" logo are trademarks belonging to
Outskirts Press, Inc.

Printed in the United States of America

Acknowledgements

I am fortunate to have the friendship of good writers like Jim Fetler and Joe Gallo who have given me both encouragement and insightful critiques. I am grateful to my neighbor, Nancy Tector, for her illustrations of Windy Nell and Don Quixote. And I am especially blessed to have the loving support of my wife, Elsie, who is able and willing to make candid observations that never (well, hardly ever) go unheeded.

Contents

Introduction

Call it what you will. It might be occasional verse that you read at a dinner party on a special occasion. For me it's something I write only occasionally. I deliberately use the term "verse" instead of "poetry" because I do not have the temerity to put myself in the same class with poets. It's not that I am modest—it's just that I don't want to set up false expectations. To me, poetry implies something uplifting with complex metaphorical meaning that rings with beauty at the sound of the words. Verse, on the other hand, is just fun to read, and especially fun to read *aloud.* That's what I hope you will do with these lines of what-ever-they-are.

When I was a kid my parents read to me from *The Child's Garden of Verses.* I learned to love the cadence, the rhyming words, and the humor even before I understood the meaning. I have always known laughter to be a powerful educational tool and one that is often underrated. In my years of teaching I knew that if I could make students laugh, I had a much better shot at getting through to them when I wanted to make a serious point. The best success I had was when students enjoyed what they were doing. Laughter (I'm talking about wholesome laughter) opens up cerebral receptors and allows knowledge and insight to penetrate the minds of even the most reluctant learners.

All of my verses have cadence and rhyme. People have asked me if I ever write *free verse*. The answer is "not intentionally." I don't want to make the same mistake as Walt Whitman. He never made any money because all he ever wrote was free verse.

To write like Walt without a rhyme
Would make your verses last through time.
But if you want to make some cash
It's better to write like Ogden Nash.

Laughter in verse has a multiplier effect. Learning through humor helps you understand cultural references, which in turn makes it possible for you to enjoy other funny verses.

Irving Berlin could write a sonnet
About a fancy Easter bonnet.
Fourteen lines it would have to be;
A quatrain is enough for me.

While you may think this is elementary, some of my students would guess that Irving Berlin is the name of street in Germany. But if they could memorize this verse, twenty years from now I'll bet they could tell you what a quatrain is, how many lines there are in a sonnet, and perhaps even hum a few bars from "Easter Parade."

* * *

Footprints On My Tongue

I have suffered apprehension many times that I could mention
When I've muddled up the messages I've sent.
It isn't very pretty
When I'm trying to be witty
To be saying things I never really meant.

I expect that no one wonders why my accidental blunders
Come more often than they did when I was young.
It's seldom I have ever
Been so absolutely clever
As to keep from getting footprints on my tongue.

I know I'm not the brainiest when I wax extemporaneous
And I say things pretty stupid off the cuff.
As soon as I have said it
I invariably regret it,
And my apology is never quite enough.

Now, I can't become a sage by simply reading from a page
Or reciting lines of poetry I've clipped.
But I'd appear to be much brighter
If I had a decent writer,
And my impromptu lines were written in my script.

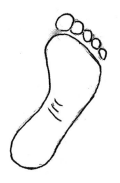

Part One
Occasional Verses

January

NEW YEAR'S RESOLUTIONS

The first of every year is when you make the resolution
to become a better person all around.
That's what I've tried to do with only moderate success,
because it's really not that easy, I have found.

I resolved that I would try to put a limit on the times
that I repeated all the stories that I tell.
Soon friends began to notice I was quiet, and they asked me
if perhaps I wasn't feeling very well.

I decided that I needed to renew my education
and behave in ways that didn't seem so callow.
Because anyone who knows me well will probably observe
that deep down I am really very shallow.

So I began perusing Schopenhauer, Nietzsche, and the rest,
and I didn't stop till all of them were read.
But now that I have finished reading all those classic works,
I can't remember anything they said.

And so another year has ended and a new one has begun;
I have advice I hope you follow to the letter.
While it might be nice to jot down all those New Year's resolutions,
a list of lower expectations might work better.

February

VALENTINE CARD

When I was a kid on Valentine's Day
my second grade teacher, Miss Amphlet, would say,
"Get out your scissors and paper and glue—"
I knew what we were about to do.

Now, don't get me wrong about making a card;
it was something to do and not very hard.
I liked to cut paper and scribble and draw,
but my cards were the worst things that ever you saw.

For starters, my writing has always been bad;
my spelling and penmanship really were sad.
I couldn't draw circles; I couldn't draw squares;
and forget about hearts, either singles or pairs.

Pasting was good; I knew how to do that
as long as the surface was perfectly flat.
And gluing was better, I'm sure you can tell;
(I probably liked it because of the smell.)

So, I'd finish the card and give it away,
and almost for sure there'd be someone who'd say,
"Isn't it lovely!—I'll cherish your song;
even though 'Valintine's Day' is spelled wrong."

But now that I'm older my methods are better
when writing a card or sending a letter.
I always use spell-check—whatever I do;
I don't have to make it with scissors and glue.

All the cards that I send now are really quite fine;
I use my computer and do them on line.
So if it's your sweetheart or maybe your mom,
it's Happy Saint Valentine's Day—dot com.

Jack Hasling

March

EVERYONE IS IRISH ON ST. PATRICK'S DAY

Everyone is Irish on St. Patrick's Day, they tell me,
but I don't believe a word of it is true.
There isn't that much Guinness to accommodate the task
of washing down those bowls of Irish stew.

If everyone were Irish, can you think what that would mean?
We'd have pennywhistles coming out our ears.
Just imagine all the Blarney that we'd have to listen to
It's enough to bring a person close to tears.

It would take a lot of Leprechauns to fill the pots of gold
that everyone expected they would find.
And the Banshees would be busy spreading curses all around
making everyone afraid to look behind.

But, of course, there is a bright side to this singular event
and everybody certainly should know it.
If it ever were to happen on some good St. Patrick's Day,
we would never be without an Irish poet.

April

THE FALLACY OF THE EASTER BUNNY

I knew about eggs—they were laid by the chickens.
I couldn't be fooled about that.
And I knew about rabbits—they were fluffy and soft
and had babies the same as our cat.

I knew about having an Easter egg hunt
and finding them out in the yard.
I figured my parents had hid them, of course,
'cause the places were not very hard.

My dad tried to tell me the bunny had cooked them
and colored them while they were hot.
Whenever he winks at my mom I'm not sure
if he's kidding, or if he is not.

I can't say I didn't believe what he said,
I just thought it seemed rather funny—
That all of those eggs painted yellow and blue
had come from a white Easter Bunny.

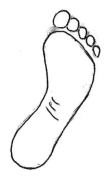

Jack Hasling

APRIL IS A TAXING MONTH

April is the time of year we gather up the facts
And check our calculations when we pay our income tax.

It isn't any fun, and very few of us applaud it
But the last thing that we want is for the IRS to audit.

The cost of running government is high, I understand,
And the debt is so enormous it's completely out of hand.

But no one wins elections, every politician notes,
By saying that they plan to tax the ones who cast the votes.

So the deficit continues to get bigger every day
And we seem to think that all the debt will simply go away.

My solution is so simple, that I hesitate to say it—
The folks who can afford it are the ones who ought to pay it.

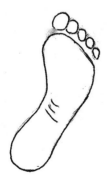

May

OH, BROTHER, ANOTHER MOTHER!

My wish on Mother's Day this year
requires some perusal,
And that's because it seems to be
a little bit unusual.
Since we have six billion people
on the planet, I would say
That maybe motherhood should take
a well-earned holiday.

I know it's good for Hallmark stock
and folks who sell you roses,
But I'm concerned about the hazards
 over-population poses.
We wouldn't have a problem
and we wouldn't feel so daunted
If every mother's child was one
 she really truly wanted.

So if parenting concerns you
 and your head is full of maybes
Then give consideration to
not having any babies.
I suspect there might have been a time
 when Eve had said to Adam,
"Let's go back into the Garden
and pretend we never had 'em."

Jack Hasling

June

MORE POMP THAN CIRCUMSTANCE

Every June in cap and gown
before the senior dance
Finds students marching to the tune
of "Pomp and Circumstance."
If Edward Elgar only knew
the cost of education
He'd have asked a lot more money
for his musical creation.

As parents we are mighty proud
of all our kids, I guess
When they receive that piece of paper
documenting their BS.
And the only thing we hope about
the sheepskin that they keep
Is that it works for them much better
than it did for someone's sheep.

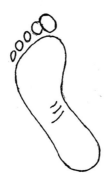

July

DAYS OF INDEPENDENCE

It's an honorable tradition
to proclaim a nation free,
And people like to tell the world
just how it came to be.
July the Fourth is known to us
as Independence Day.
In Mexico, you might recall,
it's on the Fifth of May.

The French won independence
in a really bloody deal.
Their Revolutionary day
is when they toppled the Bastille.
The English will remember
that their citizens were freed
On the day the Magna Charta
was signed at Runnymede.

The Russians have their holidays,
as anyone can see—
They celebrate the day
they overthrew the bourgeoisie.
Rome became a nation
with a destiny to last
When Caesar crossed the Rubicon
and said, "The die is cast."

The Chinese had the Boxers,
but I don't recall the date.
And the Texans had the Alamo
before they were a state.

So praise the revolutions—
that's what I'm inclined to say,
Because without them we would never get
a three day holiday.

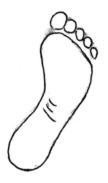

Footprints On My Tongue

August

AUGUST 6, 1945

"Take a bite," said the Snake. "You'll be glad that you did.
It's something that's good for the brain.
I know you were told it was sinful to do it,
But think of the power you'll gain.

"You'll like what you learn from this taste test you're taking—
Your knowledge will be in demand.
It's the key to discovering all that you need
To put you in total command."

Just one little bite should have been quite enough
To achieve the objective desired.
But instead there were *two* bites that led to the Fall
And all the events that transpired.

Of course, you can claim it was part of God's plan,
And surely He knew we would do it.
But we're out of the Garden of Innocence now
And there's no other way to construe it.

Once we've acquired the knowledge we have
To destroy everything in our vision.
We'd better start giving some serious thought
To who gets to make the decision.

September

AN ODE TO WORK

I must confess I'm a corny jerk
who admires the ethic known as "work."
And this is the message I want to convey
every time we celebrate Labor Day.

It's proper we pay our respects on this date,
for the sweat of our brows made this nation great.
It was work on the farm that kept us well fed
and helped us to sleep as we climbed into bed.

It was work in the factories, mines and the mills,
that gave us the means to pay all our bills.
It's work that has been our historic solution
all through the industrial revolution.

It's work that helped us all to survive;
it gave us Windows '95.
And even better than that, by gosh,
it gave us Apple and Macintosh.

Work gives us golf clubs and TV screens
and even electronic paging machines.
It helps us escape when things all go wrong
and brings us together in spirit and song.

Now my treatise on work you can tell is discreet;
I am praising the abstract and not the concrete.
By the concept of work I am truly inspired
especially now that I'm fully retired.

October

HALLOWEEN

Passing a graveyard one Halloween night,
I paused when I heard a low moan.
It was then, I concluded, without any doubt,
that I wasn't completely alone.

A Specter appeared as I stood there aghast,
believing that this was the end.
But all he apparently wanted from me
was the listening ear of a friend.

"I'm terribly misunderstood," he began,
"When everyone sees me, they run.
I'm tired of being a horrible sight;
the role of a ghost isn't fun."

"I can never conceal anything that I do.
It's a bummer," he said, " I will clue you.
The reason you can't get away with a thing
is that people can always see through you.

"And living conditions are terribly bad;
you'll never believe what I tell you.
It's amazing what real estate agents, these days,
are perfectly willing to sell you.

"I get broken-down mansions and castles and keeps
that are dirty and drafty and dark;
Never a townhouse or condo or such—
with a deck overlooking the park.

"My social life, too, is a ghastly disgrace.
That is mainly the thing that I hate.
It's almost impossible Saturday night,
when a Specter like me wants a date.

Footprints On My Tongue

"It's really unfair that I'm treated like this;
I behave myself now that I'm dead.
I don't rattle my chains or gallop around
on a horse without wearing my head.

"I quietly do my ethereal work
with modest and graceful decorum,
But nevertheless, I don't have a voice
in an open political forum.

"I'm subject to all kinds of misapprehension
as though I were some kind of fluke.
The names people call me are cruel and unkind—
like Poltergeist, Demon, and Spook.

"But since I have been in the haunting profession,
I guess I am forced to confess,
That being alive is also, I fear,
full of heartache and worry and stress."

The Shadow regarded me, then, with disdain
 and said with insightful acumen,
"I'm glad I'm a Ghost without all the fuss
and the hassles of being a human."

November

THANKSGETTING

I know I shouldn't be selfish, I guess,
however, there's something I have to confess:
Helping old ladies across the street,
giving a child a candy to eat,
Extending a hand when the table needs setting —
are things that I do for Thanksgetting.

It's perfectly clear, as we all can perceive,
it's better to give, instead of receive.
Good deeds that we do are things we can savor —
that's why I'll allow you to do me a favor.
I'll let you do something for me, and I'm betting
you, also, take joy in Thanksgetting.

Jack Hasling

December

CHRISTMAS EVE AT WAL ~ MART

It's Christmas Eve at Wal~Mart, and I'm a sentimental guy—
I must confess I get a little teary
When I wander up and down the aisles looking at the stuff
that makes me want to shop until I'm bleary.

It's such a beautiful tradition, buying things we'll never use
while the snow falls and the carolers are singing.
It warms your heart when you begin to think about the joy
that those ATM and credit cards are bringing.

So, you can set aside the sleigh bells and the holly and the cheer,
and never mind that Santa's keeping track.
For the purpose of the season, as I'm sure you'll all agree,
is to put the folks at Wal~Mart in the black.

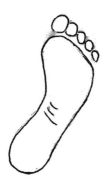

WITNESSES

So, what's the deal? They brought us here
when we were half asleep.
The shepherd always treats us like
we're just a bunch of sheep.

There's so much for us to do—
I hardly need to make pretenses—
Being counted by insomniacs
and jumping over fences.

We're not the dummies folks believe;
our job requires skill;
We must learn to find green pastures
and waters that are still.

We train the dogs to do their work
without a lot of fuss;
And it must be done so they believe
that they are herding us.

And the lamb that Mary brought to school—
the one that was so rowdy—
has a sheepskin that declares
that he's a graduate cum laude.

We're smart enough to find our way
whatever it may cost us;
The problem that we had was when
that Peep girl almost lost us.

But now I see there's something
in the valley down below;
The barn beside the landlord's inn
has taken on a glow.

16

Footprints On My Tongue

I've never seen that star before;
I thought we knew them all.
And those wise men seemed to know
exactly where the light would fall.

I have to say this new event
does give me some concern.
It makes me think that there is still
a lot we have to learn.

The shepherd says it's Christmas Eve,
and if, indeed, he's right,
I do believe that we will find
there's magic in this night.

* * *

Part Two
Christmas Letters

It's King Wenceslaus on his horse in the square

There was a time when I wrote long Christmas letters, but then my ratings began to drop. You know that's happening when you go to a friend's house for dinner and instead of your letter being posted on the refrigerator, it's lying unopened on the hall table. I started putting the letters in verse, and the ratings improved a bit. Here are a few from past years.

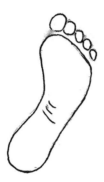

Jack Hasling

LOOKING FOR KING WENCESLAUS

Two thousand-and-three's been a pretty good year;
no hardships we have to conceal.
We've had a few bumps and some aches and some pains,
but coping is part of the deal.

We've never gone hungry; the rent's always paid
the grandkids are healthy and strong.
So with family and friends who bring joy to our life,
there's not very much to go wrong.

We traveled this year on a wing and a prayer,
and we had an adventurous trek.
We listened to languages strange to our ears—
Hungarian, Polish and Czech.

We learned a few words like "polevka" and such
and practiced a few on our group.
But instead of "Good day" as we thought we had said,
we had asked for the price of the soup.

You can never get lost in the city of Prague
you just look for the prominent statue.
It's King Wenceslaus on his horse in the square
and always he's looking right at you.

We followed the Danube while listening to Strauss,
and finally everything meshed.
It was then that we knew we had surely arrived
at the city that's called Buda-pes(h)t.

While Europe is grand with all of its charm,
coming home is even quite grander.
So keep that in mind if you're travel inclined
whenever you choose to meander.

With King Wenceslaus looking down, as he does
observing the Feast of Saint Stephen,
We pray that glad tidings, great joy and good health
will follow you all of the Season.

SANTA CLAUS DOESN'T BELIEVE IN HIMSELF

I know that you think there is never a doubt
that Santa Claus comes every year.
I don't want it whispered or bandied about,
but there may be some question this year.

I first got the word from a reindeer, you see,
who had heard the news straight from an elf,
That Santa was worried — oh, how could it be?
He didn't believe in himself?

"I'm feeling too old for this strenuous pace,"
he complained as he studied his route.
"Chimneys are narrow—there's not enough space—
I've got bunions, arthritis, and gout.

"There are six billion people out there on the road;
I hear there are more on the way.
But all that they give me to carry the load
is a sack and a tiny old sleigh."

So all of the elves, Mrs. Claus, and the deer
got behind him and gave him a lift.
"Of course you can do it," they shouted with cheer.
"It's you who was given the gift!"

"Now, Love has been born in the world," said the elves,
"to conquer our worry and fuss."

*It isn't so hard to believe in ourselves
when someone's believing in us.*

24

THERE'S NOTHING WE NEED ANY MORE

We told all our family and people we know
there's nothing we need any more.
That surely is true—at least it applies
to things that you buy at a store.

But thinking it through, we will have to admit
there is something we'd like as a gift.
It isn't a package or anything large
that might be a problem to lift.

We can save you the trouble of going down town
or shopping in some crowded mall.
The problem will be in locating the thing
that both of us want most of all.

We visited Santa—explained it to him.
We asked him to give us a clue.
"How in the world can we get what we want?
Please tell us what we have to do!"

He nodded his head in a sad sort of way
as he pondered our urgent request.
"Peace in the world is not likely this year;
there's not much demand," he confessed.

"We know you will do what you can," we replied,
"but this is the year that we need it!
Instead of a Star, there's a storm in the East.
We're hoping that someone will heed it."

"Love is the answer," he said with a sigh,
"if people are willing to live it."
One thing is certain; we all know it's true:
You can have what you want if you give it.

NOT THE BEST OF TIMES

This hasn't been the best of times,
nor has it been the worst.
There weren't a lot of blessings,
but we can't say we've been cursed.

It's been a year of stress and strain
with many grunts and groans,
But we've managed to survive these months
of wounds and broken bones.

Our travels and adventures
are reduced to almost nil.
The most excitement in our lives
is when we have to take a pill.

But fun and entertainment still
are things that we can manage—
We have a lot of laughs each time
we have to change a bandage.

The experience has truly made us
medically much wiser
And we owe it all to trips
that we have had to make to Kaiser.

All the doctors and the nurses
are familiar with our cases,
And we've come to know them mostly
on a friendly first name basis.

Our family and our friends
have come alone or in a group
And they've brought a lot of healthy food,
especially chicken soup.

So while illness isn't pleasant,
still, we know we're on the mend,
And it won't be long before we see
this coming to an end.

We are grateful for the prayers
and all the blessings that you send us
Knowing that their healing power
pretty soon will start to mend us.

We're riding on the stretcher now,
but we hope that can be changed;
We'd rather help to carry it,
if that can be arranged.

So our Christmas wish is that you stay
as healthy as you can.
Make eating right and exercising
be your New Year's plan.

Your body is a temple
and you don't want to abuse it.
While insurance might be good to have,
it's better not to use it.

SETTING THE HOUSE ON FIRE

We should really light a candle
for each blessing of the year—
We would need a lot of matches for the task.
The many things we're grateful for
have lighted up our lives—
Our good fortune has been more than we could ask.

All our grandkids have been doing things
that make us mighty proud—
They have got the stuff to know what life's about.
We have a granddaughter in college
who has earned her Gold Award
and a grandson who became an Eagle Scout.

All of them are active
in the things they like to do,
which includes about whatever you can name.
But what makes it even better,
and I'm glad I can report,
is that their grandparents are doing much the same.

We've been well enough to travel
for the first time in a year
and flew to Philadelphia for a while.
We found that pretzels on an airplane
may not be our favorite meal,
but it beats the food at Kaiser by a mile.

Now we're older and we're wiser
with more bandages and pills,
but we're grateful just to be each other's spouse.
If we lighted up a candle
for each blessing of the year,
we'd run the risk of burning down the house.

It's the loving gift of fellowship
that keeps the world aglow,
we have concluded after adding up the facts.
So we'll wish a Merry Christmas
to our family and our friends,
and then we'll not consume the world's supply of wax.

* * *

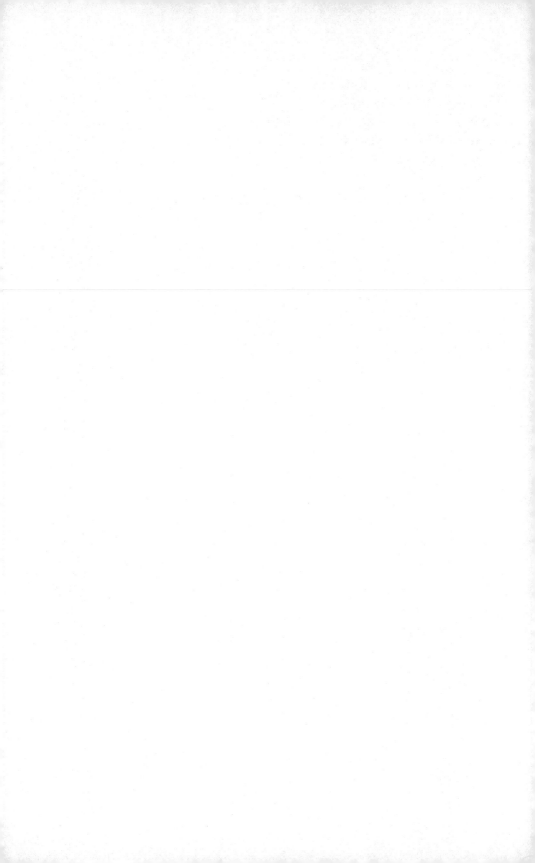

Part Three

Notes from the Coffee House

I've gotta lot o' latte in my soul.

THOSE COFFEE HOUSE BLUES

When I'm sitting at a table, and I've nothing left to lose
That's generally the time I get those coffee house blues.

I'm overdosed on caffeine; I'm on a literary roll
And you know for sure I've gotta lot o' latte in my soul.

I've got my laptop there beside me, and I've poured my second cup
So I'm settled for the evening when a stranger saunters up.

He has AirPort with his iBook and he's come to use the net
And I'd like to be as far away from him as I can get.

But he doesn't seem to notice that I just don't give a damn
So he tells me who he is, and then he asks me who I am.

Well, I pretend that I'm a writer just to make him go away
But, of course, that is exactly what he wants to hear me say.

He's got a novel he's been writing that's about the latest trend
Then he proceeds to tell the story from beginning to the end.

I smile and say politely that his book is mighty fine
But the whole time what I want to do is tell him about mine.

Then suddenly a commotion starts erupting in the place
And a guy who has a microphone is getting in my face.

It seems that I have come here at the very time I dread
Because tonight's the night when all the slamming poetry is read.

The first one is a woman and she's angry at her spouse
Who apparently is nothing but a lying, cheating louse.

Well, I'm sorry that the lady has to tolerate that crap,
But she doesn't have to dump her dirty laundry on my lap.

Jack Hasling

The next one is political and he thinks he has to shout.
He wants to overthrow the government and get the bastards out.

Well, I must admit the guy has got a pretty solid case,
But I'd like to know what other bastards plan to take their place.

So I come here when I can, and that's most any time I choose
To enjoy the melancholy of the coffee house blues.

And when I'm pecking on my laptop and I'm on another roll
You'll know for sure I've gotta lot o' latte in my soul.

CAFFEINATED INJUSTICE

I seldom find a coffee house that serves my favorite drink—
It makes me want to take their beans and roast 'em.
They really do discriminate deliberately, I think,
Against the people who'd prefer a cup of Postum.

I resent that coffee drinkers don't include me in their loop;
It's a problem, and I really want to end it.
I'd like to call a meeting of the Postum drinkers' group
But I'm afraid that there'd be no one who'd attend it.

Jack Hasling

WHERE HAVE ALL THE FOLK SONGS GONE?

Where have all the folk songs gone—
the ones we used to sing?
What happened to the spirit
that those melodies would bring?

There were songs about injustices
and causes we would settle,
 And now the only thing we hear
is rap and heavy metal.

We had Peter, Paul and Mary
and the Kingston Trio, too
Who could always lift our spirits up
before the night was through.

It's no wonder the society
has gotten so unruly
Without the lessons that we learned
from people like Tom Dooley.

We hadn't many virtues,
and a lot of us had sinned,
But we all were seeking answers
that were blowin' in the wind.

If we only had a song
that we could sing throughout the land,
We could hammer out a message
with Pete Seeger and his band.

We have to get the spirit back,
as everybody says;
We need to find a woman
who can sing like Joan Baez.

Footprints On My Tongue

The message of Bob Dylan now
could use some rearrangin';
The times, in case you haven't noticed,
need a lot of changin'.

It's really not much different
than it was in sixty-eight;
The players aren't the same,
but still the cause is just as great.

We can't expect to overcome
unless we know the tune,
And the way the world is headed now
we'd better learn it soon.

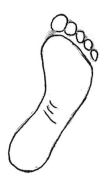

Jack Hasling

WHAT SHALL I BE WHEN I GROW UP?

When I was six or seven
I was good at climbing trees.
I could scramble onto any branch
and hang there by my knees.

I could shinny up a drain pipe;
I could swing upon the drapes.
And that's because I longed to be
like Tarzan of the Apes.

But now I know that dream of mine
was really quite insane.
I was much too young to handle
a relationship with Jane.

I could surely do the climbing
and a somersault or two
But I'm afraid I have to say,
that's mostly all that I could do.

By the time I reached eleven
I was thinking that of course,
What I'd like to be is someone
like Roy Rogers on a horse.

It's true I couldn't ride or shoot,
but that's not everything.
Most important for a cowboy
is to kiss your horse and sing.

At twenty-one I started in
assessing all my traits
And decided to be President
of these United States.

Footprints On My Tongue

I knew I had the features
other heads of state had shown,
Most important was to measure
 very high testosterone.

Now I've reached the age of seventy,
and I'd like to share my hope:
I would really be a happy guy
if I could be the Pope.

I know the pay is modest
and without gratuity,
But what makes it all worthwhile
 is the infallibility.

Lots of times some folks consider
my opinions to be odd
And I'd like to let them know
that what I'm saying comes from God.

And if they give me static
about any little thing,
I will tell them all politely
they can simply kiss my ring.

Jack Hasling

OVERCOMING SELF-ESTEEM

The reason the world is not peaches and cream
is there's too many people with high self-esteem.
Someone has told them without any doubt
that loving yourself is what life's all about.

Just do what you want if you think you deserve it—
no need to believe that you have to reserve it.
Nobody cares any more if you're sinning
as long as you get what you want and are winning.

For the smallest achievement be sure that you tout it,
and don't for a minute feel guilty about it.
What do we say to carousers and boozers?
Admitting your weakness is only for losers.

So what can I tell you about this addiction
before I attempt a prophetic prediction?
To inherit the earth is the goal that we seek,
so we better start practicing now to be meek.

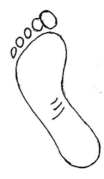

CHAPTER AND VERSE

Some want the Ten Commandments to be on the courthouse wall
Instead of all the jargonistic platitudes.

I'd rather have the Pentagon proclaim their Christian ways
With a prominent display of the Beatitudes.

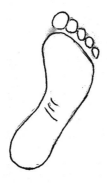

Jack Hasling

IT'S ONLY A GAME

I much prefer the game of golf to almost any other—
The philosophy appeals to me a lot.
It's important that the golfer keep an accurate account
Of every single time he makes a shot.

More important is the fact that golf's a spiritual game
That improves the better nature you display.
You must identify your errors and admit them to yourself
Or else you're destined to repeat them every day.

And because of the integrity required in the game
There's a standard that will surely never die.
Every player who has ever missed a putt will surely tell you
That, of course, we know that golfers never lie.

Yet the scoring often bothers me for reasons I'll relate:
It's the total objectivity I dread.
The change that I've suggested to my buddies on the course
Is to have a more subjective view instead.

The score is just a number that's recorded on the card,
Not the qualitative value or the distance,
I am not allowed a footnote or a verbal explanation
In spite of all my protest and resistance.

But I'll play the game and don the funny clothes you have to wear,
And I'll even sport the knickers and the hat.
Because golf is not a microcosm of the game of life—
It's a good deal more significant than that.

LIGHT IS GOOD

Light is good—especially when
I'm walking home at night
and all I see is darkness,
and there's nothing else in sight.
All the noises seem peculiar
and the spooky things go bump.
And I bark my shins upon
a nasty unexpected stump.

But light is also scary;
it throws shadows on a tree.
And it's not a comfort even though
I know the shape is me.
In the bleachers for a baseball game
and darkness starts to fall,
there must be light upon the field
before the umpire says, "Play ball!"

And in the funnies when a character
is feeling quite distraught,
a light bulb means that he has had
a really brilliant thought.
Shedding light upon an issue
is a good thing to achieve
when there's something real important
you want others to believe.

There's the existential moment
when you know a thing is right,
and you suddenly exclaim
that you at last have seen the light.
Yet, I know that secret devils
live inside the best of souls,
and we'd rather not expose them
as we play our human roles.

Jack Hasling

It's those lies that live inside us—
the ones we know are wrong—
that keep us in the darkness
and prevent our being strong.
The truth of who we really are,
we often try to hide.
But it's light that makes it possible
to see ourselves inside.

MILLENNIUM THINGS

*(On the occasion of New Year's Eve 1999
and inspired by Rodgers and Hammerstein)*

Phonograph records and e-mail and faxes
Computers and web sites and state income taxes;
Microwave dinners while watching TV;
Are things the millennium's given to me.

Monopoly players and Trivia Pursuiters,
Soccer and football and Super Bowl rooters
Viagra and Prozac and birth control pills,
The Millennium's cured almost all of our ills.

Civil Rights and—Union Workers
Women finally vote
All of these things that we now can enjoy
No longer seem — remote.

Street lights and stop lights and traffic congestion
Pills you can take to prevent indigestion
Used cars and drive-ins and flying machines
The millennium's constantly changing the scenes.

Paperback novels and satellite dishes
Digital watches and tanks for our fishes
Tacos and sushi and pizza and beer
These are the things that we'll always hold dear.

Now it's ending; soon it's over
Counting down from ten
We'll want to remember the wonderful times —
Then we can start — again.

Jack Hasling

MORALITY AND SIN

(On the occasion of the 1996 election.
The cadence may remind you of the "Wabash Cannon Ball")

Listen to the speeches
as the politicians roll;
In November we will have to pick
Bill Clinton or Bob Dole.
It's hard to choose between them;
they each deserve to win.
Bill supports morality
and Bob's opposed to sin.

Campaigns are expensive,
and they're risking every cent;
But when you're in the White House,
you don't have to pay the rent.
The one who doesn't get the job
will surely be annoyed;
'cause Bill is temporary,
and Bob is unemployed.

The wives, of course, will play a part,
and that's why they're involved;
Elizabeth has questions,
and Hillary's got them solved.
Both of them are lawyers,
and they're smart it can be said;
But I'll bet you'll never see them
wash a dish or make a bed.

The states that grow tobacco
will want to have their say;
Both candidates would rather see
the issue go away.

46

Footprints On My Tongue

If cigarettes are harmful,
should they even be on sale?
Bob says you can smoke 'em,
and Bill says, "Don't inhale."

Balancing the budget
is bound to be a test;
And neither wants his plan to be
considered second best.
But knowing how to do it
depends on where you're at;
Bill says "Grow production,"
and Bob says, "Cut the fat!"

Oh, Listen to the speeches
as the politicians roll;
In November we will have to pick
Bill Clinton or Bob Dole
It's hard to choose between them;
they each deserve to win.
Bill supports morality
and Bob's opposed to sin.

A book of verse would not be complete without a limerick. (I don't know exactly why.) I searched through all three of the ones I had written and picked this one for its educational value—geography, architecture, and medicine. It also illustrates an important form of literary verse. It was written while I was traveling in Italy and saw that amazing tower in Pisa. I read the lines to our guide, Francesca, and asked her how she liked it. She flipped me an international gesture and told me that Italian men did not have that problem.

GETTING IT STRAIGHT IN PISA

In Pisa I had a compunction
To straighten that towering truncheon.
Viagra, I think
Would fix in a wink
That Italian erectile dysfunction.

Part Four
Birthday Wishes

WISDOM

People have asked me the secret of life
and I have a remarkable plan—
Just keep having birthdays one year at a time
and do that as long as you can.

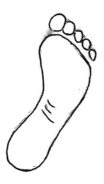

Jack Hasling

IT'S GOOD TO HAVE A SISTER

It's good to have a sister, and especially ones who's older,
to prepare you for the passages of life.
She can teach you how to dance when you're invited to a party,
and how you ought to hold your fork and knife.

She's a girl, so she's aware of things that don't occur to guys
who need to know the way they should relate.
Big sisters are the ones to give you all the little hints,
like walking on the curbside with your date.

It's good to have a sibling who can pave the way in school;
it always made me proud as I could be.
But it's tough when she is smarter and the teachers always say,
"I hope that you perform as well as she."

You can always count on sisters to include you in their games—
playing newspaper reporter was a joy.
She and cousin Mildred were the editors in chief
and I, of course, became the copy boy.

And then one day she married and became somebody's wife—
that meant she had another role to play.
Soon I became an uncle with responsibilities to bear.
I passed another milestone that day.

A sister sees you through the many stages of your life—
getting married is just one of them, of course.
And a sister can provide you with a place where you can stay
at the time when you are getting your divorce.

So it's good to have a sister for the reasons I've explained—
and one who has the wisdom of a sage.
She's a blessing and a comfort, and she's fun to be around
And that's the truth regardless of her age.

WHEN HE WAS FIVE AND TWENTY

When he was five and twenty,
he felt good about himself.
He had earned a football trophy
he could put upon his shelf.
And before he went to college
just to prove that he had brains,
He joined the paratroopers
and was jumping out of planes.

When he was five and thirty
he carried quite a heavy load,
With a wife and kids to keep him
on the straight and narrow road.
When he was five and forty
he had knowledge, he had wit;
He could understand the physics
that would make an atom split.

When he was five and fifty,
he could swim and dive and float;
He could hike and ski and, best of all
go fishing from a boat.
When he was five and sixty,
he had achieved a certain flair;
He had reached the age when he could start
collecting Medicare.

He thought when he was younger
that new wisdom would accrue
And now he's five and seventy,
and ah, 'tis true, 'tis true!

Jack Hasling

WHEN GLADYS WAS BORN IN NINTEEN-OH-FIVE

When Gladys was born in nineteen-oh-five
even George Burns was not yet alive.
The man in the White House was both rough and ready.
It was Roosevelt, yes—not Franklin, but Teddy.

There wasn't much traffic or blowing a horn;
just a few Model Ts at the time she was born.
And TV commercials were never presented;
The radio crystal had just been invented.

As bands started playing and flags were unfurled
the new Great White Fleet was sent out to the world.
We didn't imagine or even suspect
that it probably wasn't politically correct.

Japan was competing against Russian ships
instead of with us over silicon chips.
As a means of improving our national morale
we had just started building the Panama Canal.

And south of the border, the folks couldn't stand it—
they were all getting raided by Pancho, the Bandit.
There's been lots of history since nineteen-oh-five
But Gladys had managed somehow to survive.

We're glad that she lived all the years she went through
It helps us to think maybe we'll do it, too.

Part Five

Children's Stories
for Grownups

Footprints On My Tongue

The Child is Father of the Man

William Wordsworth observed that, "The Child is father of the Man." Who we were as a child determines the kind of person we become as an adult. Our parents, genetic structure, experiences, and social environment have affected us the most, but much of our character and personality was certainly influenced by what we read and what was read to us.

My grown kids, who have children of their own, have commented occasionally on my parenting. They tell me that one of the best things I did was to read aloud to them. They still remember many of the stories. Equally important, they remember the impact of having been read to. Reading aloud to kids encourages them to read for themselves; it also provides an opportunity and a venue for talking about values.

The story has to be something fun and interesting for the child and for the reader, too. I read a lot of Dr. Seuss to my kids because all of us loved the funny rhymes. I have always known the importance of rhyming words. I can still remember things that I memorized as a pre-school child.

When my wife was teaching kindergarten, I got to thinking about the opportunity for conveying more positive messages in simple children's rhymes, like jump rope chants. I don't know if children still jump rope anymore; if they do, I would like to have them memorize lines that improve their minds. The chants I grew up with were pretty stupid. "Down by the river, down by the stream, Johnny broke a bottle and he blamed it on me. I told Ma, Ma told Pa. Johnny got a licking so ha, ha, ha." And then it continues while you jump, "How many spankings did he get? 1-2-3-4 . . ." Those kinds of things stick with you all your life, and they are totally pointless. So I decided I would write some constructive jump rope chants.

Open up the magazine, open up the book.
It doesn't cost a penny just to have a little look.
You're not too old, you're just the right age.
How many words are on the page? 1-2-3-4. . .

When I was a kid I made a lot of paper airplanes. They used to have them on the back of boxes of cereal. My mother let me go to the grocery store and pick the breakfast food that had the model airplane I wanted to cut out. She'd even let me dump the flakes into another container so I could have the box right away. She was a great mom.

THE PAPER TRAIL

My name is Tony Paper;
I'm eleven inches tall.
I have a lot of cousins—
some are big and some are small.

I guess my Uncle Charlie
is the one who wins the prize.
He measures fourteen inches,
 but, of course, he's legal size.

My home is in a ream
where I have lived since just a lad.
(My single cousins choose to live
in someone's memo pad.)

You probably have guessed by now
before I start my caper—
We're a family known more commonly
as plain old writing paper.

But I became a lot more special
than a slice of cold salami
When an expert started using me
to practice Origami.

He shaped me like an ostrich
and an alligator, too.
I guess I've been most everything
you might find in a zoo.

But then one day this fellow
did a really clever thing.
He made a paper airplane
with a sweeping delta wing.

Jack Hasling

I learned to do a barrel roll
and fly an inside loop.
Then I made a perfect landing
in a bowl of noodle soup.

But the thing I have to tell you
that I'm noted for the most—
I'm the first one of my kind
to ever fly from coast to coast.

I was packaged in an envelope
and loaded on a plane;
We left from Philadelphia
in a cold and drizzly rain.

I flew to California
for the sunny western air
And I can't begin to tell you
 how much fun it was out there.

I arrived in Cupertino
and before I could unpack
Someone opened up the envelope,
and there was Grandpa Jack.

He seemed to be delighted
that I'd come to have a stay,
And he said he'd show me all the sights
of San Francisco Bay.

He put me on his bicycle
and rode me all around.
I stuck my foot between the spokes
to make a clacking sound.

Footprints On My Tongue

We pedaled to the park
which really wasn't very far.
We slid on slides and swung on swings
and climbed the monkey bar.

We visited the library
to find a special book.
He set me on the counter
where I'd have a chance to look.

And because I was so thin
it wasn't hard for me to slide
In between some of the pages
where I could see what was inside.

I met a Rabbit and an Owl,
and someone really very funny
Whose head got stuck inside a jar
while trying to lick honey.

It was Pooh Bear, and he asked me
if I'd call his neighbor, Roo
Because he had a little problem—
just doing what bears do.

I moved into another book
because I was so flat.
An Elephant was in a Tree;
a Cat was in a Hat.

I listened very quietly;
it was the thing to do.
It's not polite to make a sound
when Horton Hears a Who.

I went from book to book,
but there was one I couldn't pass;
I had to go to Wonderland
and through the Looking Glass.

I had a little cup of tea
with Alice and her friends;
You must be sure to meet them all
before the story ends.

So, I want to tell my story now
 before I get too old.
Because like every scrap of paper,
very soon I'll have to fold.

It isn't very often
that we get to tell our tale
And I'm grateful for the chance I've had
to walk the Paper Trail.

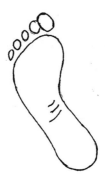

I have written several children's stories. One of them was inspired by a lecture I heard on a nature walk. I was struck by the fact that there are so many remarkable things that can be said about a creature as simple as a newt. I went home and composed a poem entitled *Salamander the Great.* As the story goes, a volume of classical stories, one day, fell off of a bookmobile. It was noticed by a literate newt named Sal:

He opened the book and spent many days
eating nothing but crackers and cheese.
And all through the night he devoured the works
of Homer and Sophocles.

It seems that Sal was of royal blood. His father was King Phil who presided over the land of Marshadonia.
He dreamed of Ulysses and Oedipus, too,
and envisioned a glorious fate—
He would conquer the world, if his destiny called,
*and become...**Salamander the Great!***

What I learned on the nature hike was that all newts are salamanders, but not all salamanders are newts. That turned out to be a bit of logic that I could use as an example when Sal consults with his friend, Aristotle the Frog.

A philosopher's job is to think of great thoughts
full of logical, helpful suggestions.
Aristotle the Frog was the one you would ask
about answers to difficult questions.

For the rest of the story you'll have to wait for the release of a children's book that will be published shortly after this one. Look for ***Salamander the Great*** and learn how he saves the worms from being "...impaled on a fisherman's hook!"

I find it great fun to write about characters in history and literature, Being the idealist that I am, my favorite is Don Quixote. I wanted to write a verse about him, but I knew I had to have a perspective that was different from that of Cervantes. Soooo...I have written it from the point of view of the Windmill.

Jack Hasling

WINDY NELL

I remember how it started
on a clear and gusty day.
They were laying my foundation
and I heard the workmen say,

"She'll be strong and she'll be steady
with a duty to perform,
And when the sails are fitted on her,
she'll be crankin' up a storm."

In the fall I was completed,
and they named me "Windy Nell"
And I lost no time in grinding up
the harvest in the dell.

Footprints On My Tongue

For the purpose of a windmill
is to turn a heavy wheel
That will mash the wheat and barley
to supply the baker's meal.

I could do the work of many,
and I didn't mind a bit.
There were times that I was gaining speed
when everyone had quit.

On a summer night at sunset
when the temperature had thinned,
The energy flowed through me,
and I got a second wind.

It was fun to be a windmill;
I could act just like a kid.
The children all did cartwheels
and tried to copy what I did.

One day a little neighbor boy
was showing off his skill.
The girl next door was watching
as he came running up the hill.

I thought he'd do a somersault,
but that was not his plan.
I felt a tug and realized
he'd climbed upon my fan.

My blade was at the bottom,
but it soon began to rise;
The little boy was carried up,
I'm sure to his surprise.

I was horrified, but no one ever
taught me how to stop.
There was nothing I could do
until he reached the very top.

Jack Hasling

I held my axle steady,
so he wouldn't lose his grip.
When you're riding on a windmill,
you can't afford to slip.

I eased him over gently,
and put him back where he had been.
I didn't want the crazy kid
to try that trick again.

To assure him I meant business
and expected him to mind,
I reached out with my other blade
and whacked the kid's behind.

Footprints On My Tongue

I don't do that very often,
but I made this one concession.
I applied a little pressure
where it made the most impression.

And to show you that I'm versatile—
you'll think it kind of neat—
That the whole time this was happening,
I continued grinding wheat.

There are stories I could tell you,
and the one I'd like to trace
Is about a knight who dreamed he'd make
the world a better place.

Jack Hasling

He would challenge every tyrant,
not for glory or for fame—
But for honor and for justice—
Don Quixote was his name.

The first time that I saw him
I could tell he was a knight.
He was dressed in all his armor
and was a most impressive sight.

He had a lance upon his shoulder
and a shield upon his knee
And how his horse could hold him up
was more than I could see.

It wasn't hard to know that
with his elegant attire
He would need to have the service
of a man to be his squire.

In a moment there appeared a figure
proving I was right;
For riding on a donkey,
Sancho Panza came in sight.

I saw them both upon a hill
and waved as best I could.
I expected they would wave to me,
as certainly they should.

But instead the Don regarded me
with a cold and distant frown.
And sitting tall upon his steed,
he pulled his visor down.

Footprints On My Tongue

Now I've never dressed for battle
or prepared for my defense,
But I could see the situation
was potentially intense.

For reasons quite unknown to me,
I was forced to take a stance
Against a knight who'd chosen me
to be the target of his lance.

He came at me with all his might
across the distant field.
I could see the sunlight flashing
on his armor and his shield.

His task, of course, was ill-advised—
the fact of that was plain;
He concluded I was evil
and a monster to be slain.

I couldn't let him do it,
though his motives were the best.
He would have to find another way
to satisfy his quest.

He pressed his charge without relent
and might have pierced my side,
But I parried with my lower blade
and made him lose his stride.

When he turned to change direction
and to take a different course,
I aimed my upper blade at him
and knocked him off his horse.

He lay there stunned until he knew
he'd finally have to yield.
His friend, the squire, came and gently
pulled him off the field.

Now I've thought a lot about that day
and all that had occurred,
And for many months I must admit
my reasoning was blurred.

Clearly he had lost the fight
when all was said and done,
But one thing that I knew for sure—
it wasn't me who'd won.

I can claim a lot of virtues
'though I know I'm not a saint.
I am strong and I'm dependable
and work without complaint.

There's not a shred of malice in me,
and I care for folks a lot,
But I can tell you this for certain—
a hero I am not.

Like all of you I'll never know
what fate there is in store.
I'd like to leave the world
a little better than before.

I live my life from day to day
with purpose, so it seems,
But Don Quixote taught us how
to dream heroic dreams!

In 1996 I published a children's story called *The Little Rock.* It was a story I had told to my daughter on a hike in the Sierra when she was eight years old, and she remembered it. When she became an adult, she urged me to write it in verse form. It was about a little rock who wanted to get bigger:

He exercised with all his strength
To increase his weight and height and length
But when he measured his rocky frame
All his dimensions were still the same.

He decided that before it was too late he'd better get some advice from bigger rocks, so he traveled around the world to places like Gibraltar and Plymouth.

A wiser rock would have, he thought
The weighty answer that he sought.
"I have to learn how rocks get taller
before erosion makes me smaller."

He even consulted with the ancient ones at Stonehenge:
The monolith explained at length
A rock's endurance is its strength.
Regardless of your cause or mission
You are part of this tradition.

But none of them could give him answers. Not even Mt. Everest. So he returned to his cave only to find that men were chipping away at the rocks with a pick. Well, the Little Rock was *petrified.* Finally he discovered the truth.

The Little Rock learned that sure enough
He was a diamond in the rough.
And folks would come and say with awe,
"That's the BIGGEST ROCK I ever saw!"

Well, the Little Rock was placed in a museum. The following story is the sequel when he finds that he has a kindred soul.

Jack Hasling

THE LITTLE ROCK MEETS ROSETTA STONE

I'm sure that you'll remember
to the wonderment of all
The "Little Rock" turned out to be
most anything but small.

He was revealed to be a diamond
of the very rarest kind
And the experts who discovered him
delighted in their find.

He was regarded as a treasure
and got lots of close attention;
The museum's advertisements
always gave him special mention.

The people came from miles around
to see this precious gem,
And residing in his case of glass,
he looked mighty big to them.

He enjoyed the "oo's and ah's"
and while his spirits often soared,
There were times when he admitted
that he got a little bored.

The guards were nice and so were all
the visitors and such,
But as for fun and recreation—
well, there wasn't very much.

So I'll reveal to you his secret,
and I don't intend to shock,
But the Little Rock was very smart
and learned to pick his lock.

Footprints On My Tongue

At night when it was quiet
and he couldn't hear a sound
He'd slip out of his case
and then proceed to look around.

He'd tiptoe down the hall
as much as any rock was able,
And hop upon a statue
or a window sill or table.

And that is how he chanced to meet,
when she was quite alone,
A kindred soul whom all the world
had called "Rosetta Stone."

Rosetta was a charming girl,
and also very smart.
She was extremely good at languages
and learned them all by heart.

It was fun to talk to Rosie;
it was a joy to hear her speak,
Telling stories in Demotic
or Egyptian or in Greek.

It was she who could decipher
all the hieroglyphic words
That were written by King Ptolemy
and other ancient nerds.

She kept records for the Pharaohs
when they had duties to discharge,
And she became the royal memo pad
on Cleopatra's barge.

You would think that she'd be proud
of all the kudos she'd collected,
But her scholarly accomplishments
were not what she expected.

She was well advanced in letters,
and in sciences, and art,
And in matters academic
she could always to do her part.

Rosie wanted more than anything,
before she got too old,
To engage in occupations
that were daring, brave, and bold.

To be heroic in her ventures
and to be the single spark
That would help to free a nation—
like the Saintly Joan of Arc.

She said, "I'd like to know what happens
when an army takes the field.
I could be a sword for Joan of Arc,
or possibly her shield.

I could protect her in the battle
when she was fighting all alone;
I could play a more important role
than just a chiseled stone."

She discussed this with her confidant
and friend, the Little Rock
In the early morning hours—
about one or two o'clock.

Footprints On My Tongue

It was then that all museum guards
were home asleep in bed
And the artifacts could listen
to what one another said.

The Little Rock could understand
what Rosie was expressing.
"There was a time," he said, "I thought
the world was really quite depressing.

But it's not what happens to you
or the placement of your star;
It's your reaction to the circumstance
that makes you what you are.

The French are sure to tell you
just exactly what it means
That the savior of their country
was the Lady from Orleans.

But the Maid did have her problems
which created quite a stir
Especially when her captors
made it really hot for her."

"That's precisely what I mean,"
exclaimed Rosetta with a groan.
"No one could have burned me up,
because I'm made of stone!

I could have saved the day at Rouen—
I don't have any doubt.
I could have stomped upon the burning coals
and put the fire out."

"That may be true," the Little Rock
replied with some admission
"But to be a sword or shield is not
a practical ambition.

"I'm afraid you'd be too heavy
in your present massive state;
If you'll excuse my being candid,
you'd have to lose a little weight.

"Besides," her friend continued,
"it's quite easy to construe
That you can make the world a better place
by doing what you do.

"The impact of your talents
has been studied far and wide;
I could show you some examples,
if you'd let me be your guide."

Rosetta Stone agreed to take
a tour through all the halls
And examine the exhibits
that were housed within the walls.

"There is much to see,"
the Little Rock related at the start,
"And then you can decide
where you would like to play a part.

"Let's look into the armory—
that's a good place to explore,
Where the soldiers in medieval times
displayed their tools of war.

There are knives and swords and axes—
even crossbows and the like;
There's a mace and there are lances
and a spear that's called a 'pike.'

"The noblemen and princes
wore the armor that you see;
When they dressed themselves for battle
they were all that they could be.

"It surely was exciting,
without making any jokes,
But you see," the Little Rock explained,
"they also killed a lot of folks."

Rosie truly was impressed
with what the Little Rock had said,
Maybe soldiering was not for her—
but something else instead.

Her companion led her down to where
the models were displayed
And showed to her historic scenes
dramatically portrayed.

There was a library in Egypt
that was the finest in the state.
It was build by Alexander—
that's one reason he was Great!

It contained the books of Aristotle
written all by hand,
As well as works from other famous
scholars in the land.

Rosetta was delighted with
the things that she had learned,
But she was saddened to discover
that the library had burned.

"What we need," the Little Rock explained to her,
"is people who can write.
It's too bad we have so many
who do nothing more than fight."

Again Rosetta got the point
and nodded affirmation,
And she listened more intently
to the Little Rock's narration.

He said "There's one invention
that the world will always bless."
And then he showed her
Johann Gutenberg's amazing printing press!

Well, Rose was overwhelmed
by this discovery of the age.
It seemed that in her book of life
she'd turned another page.

She said, "There's something there
that I have just begun to see.
This printing press appears to be
remarkably like me."

"You're right," her friend replied
as he confirmed her observation.
"But I'm sure you see that there is
one important variation.

"All the letters used in Johann's press
will move from frame to frame.
However, yours, I fear, are carved in stone
and always stay the same."

"But I'm part of a tradition,"
said Rosie, trying not to spoof.
"I'd be the first in my profession
who could make a galley proof!"

When she saw her friend was skeptical,
she added with wink,
"The only thing I'd need
is just a little printer's ink."

The Rosetta Stone a printing press?
It's more sensible, of course,
Than thinking that you're armor
for a lady on a horse.

And besides, because of Rosie,
and the letters on her face,
We understand each other better,
and the world's a nicer place.

* * *

ENDINGS

Endings are good but beginnings are better—
There're lots of ideas I can borrow.
As soon as I can
I'll come up with a plan
And start writing verses tomorrow.

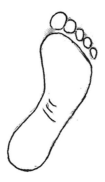